POEMS OF CHILD ABUSE,
MENTAL ILLNESS, SUICIDE,
GRIEF AND SEX.

For Phil.
They are always for you, my patient
man.

First Edition: 2021

ISBN 9798514547494

With heartfelt thanks to Microsoft Word help files which prevented me from throwing my laptop out of a window while putting together the sound file for Lament For a Horse.

For more information about other exciting near misses with frustrating technology find me on

TWITTER: @thepontypoet
INSTAGRAM: @thepontypoet

Praise for The Changeling Child and the Horse

A raw, powerful, and bloody brilliant collection that will stay with you long after reading.

- Dee Montague @griefpoet

The changeling child is a work of both tragedy and love, that emotionally depicts a survivor's struggle in a way that is elegant in form and raw in feeling.

- Chloe Sawyers-Rees @ChloeValTopia

Dee Dickens explores the theme of abuse through breathtaking poetry. The way this collection looks at coping mechanisms, the lasting effects that this behaviour has and ways of trying to survive are nothing short of stunning. This story of the horse and the Changeling Child is not one to be missed.

- Joe Thomas @joefishthomas

Challenging, insightful and heartbreaking; Dee Dickens poetry invites the changeling child in every reader to rise, survive and ultimately thrive.

- Sam Skelton @spanguelle

Contents

Contents

Introduction

"Real changeling vibes here mum" was the off the cuff remark from my daughter person while looking at a picture of me with my two sisters. Little did they know that it would prompt the collection for this assignment. I decided to write a collection of poems in a narrative arc describing the journey of an autistic child who was abused, and the idea of writing about myself as a changeling child was born. Sketching the first draft of the poem Escape at my writers' group had given me the context for the story as the prompt for that week was to write about an animal. I chose a horse as nine-year-old me was often found 'galloping' down the road on an imaginary steed. I decided that I would try and use form and sound, to illustrate the various emotions and situations and my Autistic Hyper Fixation joined in the conversation. This led to my not just using different forms for the different poems but researching which would pay due homage to the origins of said form. For example, in the Ode to a photograph, I wrote using Sapphic Stanzas as an acknowledgement of Ode to a Grecian Urn by John Keats. A future project will be to write one in Greek because the inflections in English make it extremely hard to do well, but that project is for after I have learned Greek. Below are two of the poems I thought worked particularly well. I will be explaining how I wrote them, why I wrote them and who influenced me. I shall also endeavor to afford a glimpse into the neurodivergent poet's process and aims.

Sonnet to Trying So Hard

I used the form of a sonnet as they are closely associated with the idea of the 'love poem'. The name of Sonnet 18 by William Shakespeare may not be something that evokes romance, but there are few who do not recognise the first line. "Shall I compare thee to a summer's day? Thou art more lovely and more temperate" (Shakespeare, 1609). Another recognisable opening sonnet line is Elizabeth Barrett-Browning's How Do I love thee? Let me count the ways (Barrett-Browning, 1850). Both sonnets use lower case 'r' romantic with flowery language, yet Christina Rossetti wrote in a more melancholy tone with Remember (Rossetti, 1862) being about love after death. I inserted the line 'Once more into the breach" as a nod to Shakespeare's Henry V (Shakespeare. 1599) and to show the Changeling Child was going to war with the world. I have stayed true to the sonnet traditions of love and flowery language while updating the idea of love to something more modern.

I also chose this form because the rhythm of iambic pentameter brought to mind the sound of a horse galloping. The da-dum, da- dum of the hooves follows the form of an unstressed syllable followed by a stressed one. Musician Chris Rea talks about the phenomenon in Steam Train Blues (Rea, 2005) and how the sound of the trains influenced the music. I found that there is a musicality in poetry that lends itself to this kind of experimentation. I used Heroic Couplets not just because the rhyming was a challenge, but because the Changeling Child and the Horse are riding into battle as heroes of their own story. Once I settled on the form, and to have the iambs in each couplet of the sonnet rhyme with each other, the process was slow and sometimes frustrating, but ultimately rewarding. Much like breaking a horse. To represent this, after it was written, I added in punctuation to slow the poem down in some places and speed it up in others. For instance, in the last two lines we have her galloping with no punctuation until the end "She tries and fails and sleeps and wakes and then" (line 13) which is ten syllables without a breath that transports the reader to racing with the wind in their face, until we stop, tired and the last line "so tired, she quails and weeps and breaks again" (line 14) leaves us slowed down and breathing heavily, much like a horse after a long run.

John Keats coined the phrase 'Negative Capability' to describe the "life of sensations rather than thoughts" (Keats, 1817), "not as a pejorative, but to convey the idea that a person's potential can be defined by what he or she does not possess – in this case a need to be clever, a determination to work everything out" (Hebron, 2014). Keats rejects the idea that there must be a "relentless search for knowledge" (Hebron, 2014), instead stating that the poet would "do well to break off from his relentless search for knowledge, and instead contemplate something beautiful and true" (Hebron, 2014). I would take this thinking a step further and suggest that rather than the "sense of Beauty (overcoming) every other consideration" (Keats, 1871) the knowledge of form rhythm and sound is a tool to be used to mine the beauty rather than have it passively seep into the poet's pen.

Synesthesia in poetry is "a blending or intermingling of different sense modalities" (Poetry Foundation, date unknown). For example, Charles Baudelaire in The Ragpickers' Wine, where he writes of "the dazzling, deafening debauch / of bugles" (Baudelaire, 1857, line

22) the synesthetic effects include "textual amplification, complication, and richness" (Poetry Foundation, date unknown). To simplify, poets employing synesthesia in their poetry are being clever with words to evoke a different state of understanding. Deafening is a word we might ordinarily associate with bugles, yet dazzling and debauch evokes a mood of brightness, happiness, and drunken fun. My situation is slightly different. I have medical synesthesia, where stimulating one neural pathway opens another so when I read *How Do I Love Thee?* I hear a backing track of soaring violins. *Remember* is more in the tone of a solo cello. Sonnet to Trying So Hard is a melancholy sonnet where the recipient of the love is the protagonist herself. It is a flute over muted timpani drums. This also gels with the rhythm of a horse going to war. It also allows me to 'feel' the overall mood of a poem as I write it. The Changeling Child and her Horse rushed headlong into some situations and slowly into others. The poem shows this in the rhythm, punctuation, and content.

Plosive

Repetitive body movements or repetitive movement of objects is referred to as self-stimulatory behavior or stimming (Legg, 2018). It can take many forms, "including visual, sound, smell, touch, taste, and balance and movement" (Legg, 2018). When it is verbal, it falls into the realm of Echolalia. Repeating words and phrases out of context is a good indicator that it is occurring, but it is by no means the only way it presents (Legg, 2018). My echolalia means that I enjoy saying certain words over and over as they feel good in my mouth. It also presents as my choosing words to say that are in context but are fun. For instance, rather than say many, I would use the word plethora as it makes the tip of my tongue physically tingle.

My poem Plosive was inspired by a conversation in a prompt group about how P words are the most fun to say. As poets are wont to do, we challenged each other to write a poem featuring the letter P. After a free write of all the P words I could think of in two minutes, I narrowed my choices down to five. Once I had chosen the words, I decided to use other P words as a way to inform the theme of the poem. My echolalia means that when I say a word I enjoy that I hear it more fully. To me, words that begin with P sound breathless and exciting, so it was perhaps inevitable that I would write the poem about another favourite P word, penetration. The excitement also apparent to me at least, suggested that this would be delayed, and the protagonist would be impatient. Then there is the tingling on the tongue previously mentioned. This poem was always destined to be about physical pleasure.

On deciding what kind of poem I would write, I landed on a sestina for three reasons. One, was that it would provide opportunity for my P words not to become subsumed in the stanzas, they would all be prominent. Secondly because of their origin. The sestina has been around since the 12th century and is credited to troubadours, travelling musicians and poets, specifically Arnaut Daniel. The word troubadour conjures up images of bawdy taverns and that hint at rampant sexuality meant that it fitted my theme perfectly. The third reason was that it is French in origin and therefore a challenge to master in the English language. My neurodivergent brain relished the idea of taking six words and using them in a different context all through a poem. For example. The word paper does not evoke excitement on its own, yet in the first stanza it is something to be immersed in, taking away attention, full of news of other people. In stanza two, the fly paper is sticky and irresistible, in three, the paper is the skin, ready to be written on, but delicate. In the fourth stanza the paper represents a covenant between two people. It is intimate and resonant of a wedding ceremony. Stanza five has the paper as lips, the covenant is sealed with a kiss. In six, they present themselves to each other as gifts to consummate the act of commitment. In the second envoi we have the paper burning. This evokes ideas of a bonfire which in turn makes us think of pagan weddings. The couple in this poem do things their own way, but essentially, they burn for each other. The Complaint of Lisa by Algernon Swinburne is about unrequited love and has the same feeling of desperation. He achieves this by using the word breath in a similar way. In stanza four, he uses enjambment to suggest that the absence of love and dreams causes the absence of breath and even that is not as bad as the absence of the subject of Lisa's affections.

"Without love, without dreams, and without breath,
And without thought, O name unnamed! of thee" (lines 47 and 48)

Having breath as an ending word rather than one more typical of love poetry, such as dreams, evokes the breathiness of the 'heaving bosom' which seems to be a prerequisite of women in love with a "Great king, glad lover" (line 111) who "Aye, all day long he has no eye for me" (line 121). One of the perhaps unintended effects of this poem being a double sestina is that it is also resonant of how writers of the age portrayed women. The sum of the parts of this poem suggest a wordy woman with a heaving bosom who cannot act outside the bounds of the social mores of her age. My poem is more up to date. My protagonist has no hesitation in telling the object of her affection exactly how she feels.

Incidentally, Swinburne's poem, with its summer imagery and meadow filled language prompts the music of Pachelbel's Cannon in D by Johann Sebastian Bach, whereas mine, with its closeness fills my synesthete mind with the sound of meadows and wind blowing through long grass.

Of course, no two minds, much like no two poems are exactly alike, so where I hear a cello, someone else might hear a trumpet, or nothing at all. These are some of the challenges and joys that writing in specific forms and using specific language to evoke a specific thought or feeling. That I might fail to prompt the exact same responses to my work is not discouraging. I want my reader to feel something, whether or not they take the time to interrogate exactly what that is. I would hope that this being the case, Keats would approve.

The Villain and Elle

the creaking of her bedroom door
the smell of cigarettes and sweat
hated and feared since she was four

the growling voice, *petit, amour.*
the desperate plea *not yet, not yet*
the creaking of her bedroom door.

stubble makes her mouth feel sore
she cries, he strokes her hair, his pet
hated and feared since she was four.

scream in her throat *no more no more*
his legs spread hers, his eyes a threat
the creaking of her bedroom door

she reaches for teddy on the floor
grips tight as his weight pins her, breath
hated and feared since she was four

he kisses her, then whispers, *whore.*
she lies still, numb, hot, wet
the creaking of her bedroom door
hated and feared since she was four.

Sestina for a Changeling

She wondered if she were a changeling
if that was why they couldn't love
her, if there was another child
somewhere, waiting for rescue
that never came, the light
of the doorway terrifying her.

She thought fondly of the other her
hoped she knew she was a changeling
that one day, she would embrace the light
that one day she would understand love
that one day there would be a rescue
that one day, she wouldn't be a child

and if she ever had a child
the changeling would die in order to protect her
her daughter wouldn't need a rescue
too loved to be an unwanted changeling
her child would be surrounded by love
they would dance joyfully together in the light

the other her, could not bear the light
she would always remain a child
who only knew a twisted love
that started with kisses and ended in pain, her
thoughts merged with the changeling
and they both prayed for rescue

undeserving of rescue
cowering from the light
she prayed she was a changeling

awful child, terrible child
all the things he whispered to her
love

love
undeserving of rescue
all the things he whispered to her
cowering from the light
awful child, terrible child
she prayed she was a changeling

love
cowering from the light

undeserving of rescue
awful child, terrible child

all the things he whispered to her
she prayed she was a changeling

The "Accident"

She grew older and sought to conspire
to deny him his twisted desire
He threw her on a couch
with a scream and an ouch
and then set the sofa on fire

The Emptiness

In burns unit she had envisaged
That everyone would come to visit
She waited in vain
and nobody came
to gaze upon her crackling visage.

The Breaking Point

and so this young girl from our ends,
who had not a single true friend.
her mind broken, dented,
a horse, she invented
to stay by her side till the end.

The Fallout

We sometimes saw her in the street
with nothing upon her small feet
Galloping round
Making strange equine sounds…
I regret not making more of an effort with her.
I mean, I could have said *hello* to her.
I'm Sorry.

Escape

Once upon an ancient time
there was a child of tears
who didn't belong anywhere,
was chased by dreams and fears.

Tired of never fitting in
the changeling child would cry
and try to find a way back home
or she would surely die.

One day she visits her friend the horse
and asks permission to ride

Of course says the horse
not a problem,
won't you come inside?

she climbed through a
tiny hole in the wall
they chatted the night away.

if only she can
open the door
they'll leave at break of day.

There's a push and a nudge,
it will not budge
she's run out of ideas

she finds a box of matches
and all becomes quite clear

In the corner of the barn
right beside the door
she sets a fire until the way
is blocked for them no more.

She climbs upon the horses back
alas it is too late
for the changeling child
with a dress of flames
who just wanted to escape.

Sonnet to Trying So Hard

Unto the breach dear friends! She deigns to strive.
Path true, she'll reach world's end, though pained, alive.
They range the wilds, hunt game, and plan their course.
The Changeling Child, her flame dress, and her horse.
The battle won or lost; they drink to health.
The latter costs, she can't escape herself.
It matters not she dreams which roads she'll roam,
in tatters, lost, it seems all roads lead home.
She thinks that she can stay, endure with pills.
She drinks and sees the way to cure her ills.
She prays and hopes, declares her final breath.
She plays with rope; she swears to find her death.
She tries and fails and sleeps and wakes and then,
so tired, she quails and weeps and breaks again.

Ode to a Photograph

Looking out, two pairs of eyes, green, yet dark hued.
smiling mouths, teeth bared against the world, you'll see
hands held, hair no match for the wind, the two,
the changelings hold fast.

Gripping sand held between toes,
universes beheld in each other.
The changelings hold love.

Memories of later, a room lit by starlight,
Warmth, gentleness, oneness, letting go, passion
Two lives, one breath, closeness changes meaning
The changelings hold space.

Haiku For a Changeling

When your twin leaves you
Cherry blossom underfoot
Still contains   perfume

Secrets and Grief

For Diana

When the person who knew your Very Worst Thing,
held imagined sin in the palm of their hand,
clutched your darkest moment to themselves,
cradled with love is dead,

held imagined sin in the palm of their hand,
it burns. It consumes,
cradled with love is dead,
burrows its way into your skin disguised as grief,

it burns. It consumes,
sits on your eyes and when you sleep
burrows its way into your skin disguised as grief,
weeping for you, tears seeping to ears

sits on your eyes and when you sleep
will never again hear that voice say
weeping for you, tears seeping to ears
I'm sorry.

When you die, there will be no one left who knows.
Your darkest moment will float with your ashes.
The wind will change and blow your shame
back into their faces.

Your darkest moment will float with your ashes,
back into their faces.
They will sneeze your secret and not even know.
When the person who knew your secret is gone.

They will sneeze your secret and not even know.
It will try to be told to someone else.
When the person who knew your secret is gone.
Your secret fears forgetting.

It will try to be told to someone else.
If nobody knows, did it happen at all?
Your secret fears forgetting.
I'm sorry.

A Horse Walks Into a Bar

After Tyrone Lewis

Hey.
Wanna hear a joke?

What do you call a horse who lives next door?
A Neighbour!

Horse tries to run away,
it's a terrible tale of WHOA!

Horse walks into a bar,
barman says "Hey"
horse says "Yes please"

A horse walks into a bar.
The barman offers a glass of water,
Horse says, I'm not drinking that,
this is not an idiom, it's a joke.

You get that the horse is just me right?
That I am the joke?
Ok. So.

A horse walks into a bar
and the barman says,
Why the long face?
PTSD says the horse.

Horse walks into a bar.
Fucks the first stranger
who buys it a drink.

A horse walks out of a bar;
catches sight of itself
in a shop window.
Doesn't eat for three days.

A horse falls in love with the first
horse to show it some attention,
because of course it does.
Why wouldn't it?

A horse gets changed mid-stream.
Is sure that it must have been
something it did. Shaves it's
mane off.

Horse goes into therapy.
Spends the first session
comforting the therapist

A horse bolts.
Stable door gets closed.
Horse is relieved
it can't return to a burning barn.

A horse feels the wind
in its face.
Horse has dyspraxia, trips over.
Horse breaks its leg, gets shot.

A horse dies.
Still gets flogged.

Horse goes home for Christmas

Is warned not to be
controversial. Spends the whole time
throwing up everything it eats.

Grandad turns up to Christmas dinner
horse tells him to stay away.
Family turns on horse.
Horse storms out.

Horse's family stages intervention.
Tries to tell it
that grandad is just old
he's from a different time
he's harmless really.
Horse stops eating.

Horse lies on a bed of hay
fantasizing about how
flammable it is.

Suicide Attempt Two

Slumped over saddle
With one last glance at the moon
She rides off the cliff

Plosive

My lips feel the pulsing
on the inside of your wrist as promised
by your look. You put your paper
down, your pyjamas
barrier to the pleasure
of seeing your body. Damn, please

for the love of god, please,
take them off. My blood is pulsing,
racing with anticipated pleasure.
The promise
of what is under your pyjamas,
traps me, a fly on honey paper.

Wrist skin thin as paper,
tongue tracing a word, please.
Hand reaching down to where pyjamas
cling to the pulsing,
the promise
of pleasure.

Yes, the promise of pleasure;
my tongue the pen, your body the paper
the promise
to be yours, only yours, to please
you, my body yours, my cunt pulsing,
breathless, impatient at your pyjamas.

Rip them off, those useless pyjamas.
Take your pleasure.
Slide into me, pulsing.

Our lips the paper
on which is written the promise to please
each other. Desperate to promise

each other. Promise
that there are no pyjamas
that can thwart our mission to please,
to pleasure.
Our skin the gift paper
wrapping racing blood. Pulsing,

flushed without breath, we still whisper, *Promise.*
One thought only, *Pleasure.*

Burn them, burn the ridiculous pyjamas,
watch them curl and float like paper,

then pin me down, my darling. Please.
Can't you feel the inside of my wrist pulsing?

Bad Things Are Going To Happen

After Ellen Bass

Bad things are going to happen.
You will get your heart broken
by someone who will deny they
ever held it in their hands.

Bad things are going to happen.
You will have to deal with idiots
who think coronavirus is caused
by 5G,
or the 'Lady Chemicals' that are released
when someone's tongue
knows its way around your clit.

Bad things are going to happen.
Avril Lavigne will actually die.
Again.
Britney Spears will murder her clone.
The moon landing will be proved to be real.
The moon will be proved to be real.
911 will have been an inside job.
Barak will admit he is Kenyan.

And we will have nothing to talk about;
except art, and music and poetry and
we will have nothing to do;
except write poetry and paint and
sing. Sing. Sing.

How to Write an Elegy

After Paul Tran

An elegy uses formal language and structure,

She reads all the obits, looking for his name.
she finds it she just can't, she shuts the paper.
Fell asleep, mocking the tip of her tongue.
Passed peacefully burned on the inside of her retina.

It may mourn the passing of life & beauty
In her throat, the cries of all who mourn him
selective memory writes flowers from family only
Beauty is truth and truth beauty
celebrate the life of. He
hurt me you know. And I'm sure he hurt others.
If truth is beauty then let me shine
   if a death must be mourned, let it then be mine.
He killed me countless times.

or someone dear to the speaker
I'm not afraid of his ghost.
He was always there, on the radio
when they played the song he hummed
when he was in a good mood.
The one that made me resist bedtime.
He was there in the crack of light through a doorway.
Hiding in the texture of a valentine's day teddy.
In the smell of burning flesh.

    It is a type of lyric & focuses on expressing emotions or
thoughts.

My grief is coating my lungs black
its smell sticks to my hair
turns my fingers yellow. I
shouldn't want it yet
I greedily breathe it in.

It may explore questions about nature of life & death or immorality of soul.

I wonder is there life after life
if I can expect to live after my death.
Is it the end of him?
I hope it isn't, I wish him suffering.
I wish him knowing that in the end
he was not a good man.
I am not a good woman.
He was my maker, and I don't want
to meet him again.

It may express the speaker's anger about death.

So I write another poem as memoriam
to a changeling and the horse she rode away on
and I am not sure if I am attending the funeral
for me, or to check he's actually gone.
And if one more person asks me
how I feel, I will rise up a gorgon
turn them to stone, reduce them to rubble,
use them to build a temple to resilience.

elegiac meter sounds like waves,

Let my work rise in six steps, fall back in five –
you could link this one to the sea.
Maybe have the ashes being scattered in water
Call it catharsis if that makes you feel better
Call it pollution as the flowers float away, pity
the fish who now swim with him
resist the urge to dive in after him,
gather him up, spit on him
on your way home, drop him in a bin.
Because fuck him.
Because fuck the state he left you in.
Because fuck everyone who left you with him
because fuck being the altar on which he sacrificed
your childhood.
because fuck your childhood
because fuck
because
fuck

An elegy uses formal language & structure.

Lament For a Horse

After This Mortal Coil

Long ago I felt your warm breath
When I needed strength to smile
ran my hands through mane a flowing
Climbed your back and sat astride
And you ran
ran for me, ran for me
Let me carry you
you can ride, you can ride
Always I'll hold you

Did I dream you ran wild with me?
Were you here when I first burned?
Now my embers, quenched with longing
Is a lesson both have learned
For the fire
Burns for us, burns for us
never extinguished
Oh my heart
Oh my heart shies from the anguish

I know full well I have to let you go
heart is breaking as I speak
Should I keep you in a stable
or should I offer you release?

Hear me sing
Run for me, run for me
Let me release you
Here I am, here I am.
Always I'll love you

Advice For My First Born

So many people want to try
to tell you hush, you shouldn't cry,

but one thing that I know for true,
is that crying is quite good for you.

You'll grow into a perfect child
sitting quiet or running wild.

Scrapes and grass stains on both knees
chasing birds and counting bees.

Spit covered tissue to wipe your face
never be afraid to take up space

Never be scared to hold your line
screaming no will always be fine.

Don't forget you have beauty too
but it isn't the most interesting thing about you.

Your smile is the sun, warming my heart
but remember to scream if it falls apart.

Don't hush my baby, let it all go
mamma loves you even so.

Ghazal For a Patient Man

I once feared love, a
rabbit heart,

a take a fuck
and grab it heart.

you smiled,
claimed it, heart

was struggling to
escape, run for it heart,

caught, you grabbed
fear and killed it. my heart

thanks you.
so do I, my heart.

Epilogue

And so it came to pass one day
the changeling child, she passed away.
she knew true love
it wasn't enough
she took her own life anyway.

Notes on the poetic forms used

The Villain and Elle

Collection opens with a villanelle that details how the changeling child is being abused. I chose this form as it is stark and repetitive and illustrates abuse as a cycle that doesn't end.

Sestina For a Changeling

I used a sestina here to denote the thought process. The repetition of the words is used to show the repetition of a child's thoughts. How adept they are at mulling it over and looking at the same idea from different angles This poem is about duality, of transference and coping mechanisms of children. How compartmentalising can save lives.

The "Accident", The Emptiness, The Breaking Point, The Fallout

Limericks are traditionally jokey. They have off colour humour and certain traditions such as beginning "There was a young girl". They are used to tell bawdy stories and I chose them as a form to show ease the reader further into them the darkness. Also, it is a trauma response to make light of horrific events, and this represents that well. The Fallout subtly foreshadows the ending.

Sonnet to Trying So Hard

I used the form of a sonnet as they are the first thing that springs to mind if you say 'love poem'. I also chose this form because the rhythm of iambic pentameter brought to mind the sound of a horse galloping. The Changeling Child is trying to practice self-love, but in actuality she is galloping towards her first suicide attempt.

Ode to a Photograph

I chose the ode form to describe something beautiful yet every day. Rather than talk directly about their relationship, I used talking about the photograph as a way to illustrate it, much like the Grecian Urn has a story painted on it, so the photograph tells the story of the two women. I used Sapphic Stanzas as this is traditional with an ode, but also because the young women are in love.

Haiku For a Changeling

There is something of the melancholic about a haiku and I used this form to evoke sadness and the beauty of remembrance.

Secrets and Grief

I used the sestina form here to show how the grieving mind goes in circles and repeats itself to attempt to process loss.

A Horse Walks Into a Bar

It is a truism that anything that starts with something walking into a bar is going to be a joke. I used the joke format here as there are some horrific events and images and I wanted to illustrate the tendency people dealing with trauma have to make light of them.

Plosive

Another sestina. This time to illustrate increasing desire. I also used words beginning with the letter P to make the sound of pushing, imitating the penetration the Changeling Child longs for.

Bad Things Are Going to Happen

This is an *'after'* poem and I used this concept to demonstrate that the idea that there will always be love is someone else's idea that she is taking and making her own.

How to Write an Elegy

This is an ars poetica and I used this form to show the Changeling Child comparing how she is *supposed* to do something (like grieve and respect societal grieving parameters) with how she *actually* does it. I wanted the reader to hear her voice and her anger so the ars poetica allows her to reveal her anger.

Lament For a Horse

I used a lament as it is an expression of grief. It is redolent of wailing and I wanted to show the Changeling Child letting go in a way that was authentic to her. It also gave me an opportunity to showcase her voice literally as a lament is traditionally sung, so I could record the poem in its proper form.

Advice For My First Born

I used a lullaby for this poem as the antithesis of the lullabies that told little girls to hush and let a man take care of them. I used the idea of something that would be sung to a child and therefore seep in being utilised to give good advice and avoid the trauma that the Changeling Child endured.

Ghazal to a Patient Man

A ghazal is a poem about emotion and they are usually autobiographical. I also liked the opportunity to have a poem sound like someone who is struggling to get her words out and having the last word always be the same enables some interesting enjambment to achieve this.

Epilogue

By now the reader should know. If it is a limerick, it is not going to be good news.